BRAND YOURSELF ONLINE IN 30 DAYS

5 C's to Build Your Brand

and Create Social Media Success

BRAND YOURSELF ONLINE IN 30 DAYS

5 C's to Build Your Brand

and Create Social Media Success

Stephen J. Meadows

Cronus Media Ventures, LLC

2017

ISBN: 978-0-9963197-4-4

First Printing: 2017

Cronus Media Ventures, LLC
San Antonio, TX 78240

www.CronusMediaVentures.com

DEDICATION

For my mother, Mary C. Meadows, who always believed in me and encouraged me to reach for my goals. I wish you could have lived to see my third book. I love you always!

May 10, 1948 – September 1, 2016

A special thank you to my brother, Jimmy, and his amazing wife, Elena, who were such a big help to me on this project!

As always, thank you to my dad for teaching me the value of hard work!

CONTENTS

Foreword

Stephen delivers timely and insightful information in an entertaining and practical way. By taking some of the mystery out of how social media works, Stephen encourages the reader to try new things and test their effectiveness. And I for one can certainly attest to the effectiveness of these tools in building a sustainable business. Having built a successful, non-traditional real estate brokerage myself, I launched an international online coaching company based on proven innovative marketing strategies with a heavy focus on social media marketing. Over the last 10 years, I have been lucky enough to have traveled throughout the United States training thousands of agents and small businesses on this subject; therefore, some people might say I am an expert in the world of social media for real estate. I prefer to think of myself as someone who constantly learns and shares new, helpful skills to people who thirst for knowledge. Social media just happens to be one of the topics that excites me most because it is still one of the most underutilized tools in real estate.

Fate brought Stephen and me together at American Home Shield Home Warranty where I have seen firsthand his passion for teaching and helping his agents grow their businesses. It was at American Home Shield where Stephen and I first collaborated on social media training programs as the company pushed forward with a more aggressive "added value" initiative to bring incredibly effective learning opportunities to brokers and agents everywhere. Stephen was taking what myself and other national trainers were doing on a large scale and delivering it to his agents on a local and regional level. So when I was asked to write this Foreword, there was no hesitation. I am proud to place my name along with Stephen's on this subject.

Social media, as a whole, is largely underutilized by its users, especially in the real estate market. There are countless people who either don't know where to start, how to best complete the task, or even why they should do it in the first place. Social media can be a conundrum for some people. While it is simple to access and use, it becomes deeply complex as one learns about and utilizes more and more features. The majority of users never leave the surface of the platform and leave 99% of the functionality unexplored. I always say that, "I can show agents lots of ways to win listings and convert buyers using social media, but if not done right, there are many more ways to lose listings and lose buyers!" That is why I strongly recommend Stephen's 5 C's whether you are brand new in the business or have been selling for 30 years.

The 5 C's help break down this complexity. Stephen takes topics about which there are thousands of webpages, articles, infographics, and posts, and distills them down to simple, easy-to-grasp concepts. These are concepts almost anyone can understand and utilize. His passion for training comes through on every topic. This book can definitely motivate someone to start a new social media campaign.

This book is not designed to be the definitive guide to all things social media. It's quite the opposite. This is meant to be a simplistic look at what activities can produce results. Stephen tries to find the highest return for the lowest effort. There are no high-minded, ethereal notions expressed. You don't need thousands of advertising dollars or a staff of 20 to accomplish simple, trackable goals. All you need is a desire to succeed and a little motivation to back it up.

As with any worthwhile topic, if you can just get one takeaway from reading this book, it will be worth the investment of your time. You will feel challenged to try something new, and motivated to make a meaningful change in the way you interact with your sphere of influence. It should serve as a basic template for your strategy moving forward. It is not a "one and done" read. Rather, you should keep it on hand and refer back to it on a regular basis. Use these concepts to help benchmark your own success.

If there is one thing I enjoy most when I am training a room full of eager agents, it's seeing that "eureka moment" in their eyes when I say something that resonates. This book should give you plenty of these moments. Be sure to take notes and write down the ideas that resound within you. Implement them at a pace that is comfortable, adding in new ideas as you master the one before. As you progress, do research and find more ideas on your own to apply. I guarantee that once you have a little social media success, you will be hooked and will want more!

Burke Smith

Owner/CEO, Realty ONE Group

And Founder of YourNetCoach

San Diego, CA

December, 2016

Preface

Thank you for taking the time to read this book! *Brand Yourself Online in 30 Days* is my third book, and I have enjoyed writing each new book more than the one before. The idea for this topic was actually a long time in the making. However, the final motivation to create a book out of it just sort of hit me one day like a lightning bolt, but with less pain. Three weeks later, the first draft was complete and ready for the editing process.

I have been a self-proclaimed social media junkie for many years. Some people call me a "guru." I think that title bestows too high an expectation. I prefer to see social media as my passion, rather than my calling. It's just something I enjoy immensely and, over time, something for which I have developed a skill. One of my callings in life is helping others be more successful. If you want to know what drives me, just ask for my help with a business problem and see me light up with excitement! This book represents the intersection of my passion and my calling.

In 2015, I was working for American Home Shield in southern Louisiana. My job was simple: convince real estate agents to recommend my home warranty to their customers. I was new to the area and needed a "hook" to set me apart from the competition. After 12 years of real estate sales, I have learned a few things about what matters to agents. I decided to try something new. I offered to teach a class about Facebook and LinkedIn to one of my offices. About 15 minutes into the presentation, I realized I had stumbled onto something amazing. The agents were not only listening intently, they were engaged and even excited about the information I was giving them. After a few modifications, this book was born!

It started out as a class for real estate agents to help teach them the right and wrong ways to build a social media presence. The problem was, and still is, that there are countless agents out there and only one me! I can't possibly teach this class one group at a time and make any significant difference. After all, I DO have a real job to do!

I decided it was time to write down my ideas and share them with anyone who is interested in learning more about social media. This book is not intended to be the final authority on the subject, nor will it be the last I will ever write on the subject. Social media changes far too often to have a static guide. I simply wanted to spread my knowledge and hopefully help someone make their business better!

Please know that everything in this book is from my personal experience. You may not understand or even agree with 100% of what is written here. That's not a problem. As with all my books, all I want is for my reader to walk away with at least one "nugget of knowledge." If I can teach even the simplest concept, I feel that my purpose has been fulfilled. I hope you enjoy this book and find it invaluable to your marketing efforts. I wish you all the best!

Stephen J. Meadows

Introduction

Ah, Social Media. For some, it's the greatest thing since sliced bread. For others, it's the bane of their existence. With well over 1 billion users worldwide, social media is probably one of the great inventions in the history of the human race. Personally, I find that indoor plumbing and air conditioning rank higher on that list, but social media is at least in the top ten! Never before have we been so connected or had such access to total nonsense. The amount of time I spend looking at cat memes alone is staggering!

For all its faults and distracting characteristics, social media serves a purpose. Many people use it strictly for entertainment purposes. Some use it maliciously. Others use it to make money. The latter is the topic upon which this book is focused. There are countless ways social media can be used for profit, both directly and indirectly.

This book represents a philosophy that I have developed over many years of social media usage. I don't claim that these are novel concepts, although they may be new to you. Experts in social media subscribe to similar beliefs whether they realize it or not. They are just inherently learned as knowledge and experience increases. My philosophy can be summed up with 5 words. These are what I call "The 5 C's

Social Media Success." Mastering these 5 concepts can increase your marketing effectiveness, build a lasting brand, and drive more business than ever before! The 5 C's are:

- Connection
- Content
- Consistency
- Cohesion
- Communication

As with all my approaches to training, this book is based on common sense, real world scenarios. I try to avoid industry jargon just to fill space on the page. This book will be straightforward, no nonsense, and hopefully sometimes amusing. Most of the examples will be from a real estate perspective. After all, a writer writes what he or she knows. However, these concepts apply to any business out there. It just takes a little imagination.

Chapter 1: The True Purpose of Social Media

To answer your question, NO. Social media is not all about sending game requests or taking duck-face selfies every 5 minutes. Its true purpose really depends on the user. For the vast majority, the use is purely for entertainment. Those folks have little to learn from this book. For even the most casual business user, there are 5 key elements to always keep in mind when using social media to profit. Once you have these in focus, you will begin to look at every post through new eyes. You will probably think twice on some of them.

Name Recognition

Honestly, you could probably stop reading right now, and you would have learned something. Name recognition is the most important purpose of social media. If you remember nothing else from this book, this fact will be worth the read. Everything you do on social media is to get your name out there, plain and simple. Everything else is just gravy.

Let's take a look at a Facebook Business Page, for example. In fact, let's look at mine titled, "Stephen Meadows, Coldwell Banker Brand Ambassador." The name says everything I want to convey: who I am, what I do, and for whom I do it. Every time I publish a post, my page name is associated with that post. When Jill likes my post, her friends see, "Jill liked Stephen Meadows, Coldwell Banker Brand Ambassador's post." When she shares it, they see my name as well. I probably don't know the majority of Jill's friends, and they probably don't know me. The point is that my name is out there in front of more people simply because I posted something that was of passing interest to Jill.

When choosing your content, the goal is for the post to be "likeable" and "shareable." That will ensure maximum reach. Consistently posting content that is engaging will build your influence. Soon enough, people will remember your name, and they may not even know why.

Brand Recognition

Every business has a brand, whether or not they realize it. Branding is, essentially, what you are known for. In real estate, many people call it a "niche." Whatever words you use to describe it, it all amounts to the same thing. In the competitive world of sales, it's vital to differentiate yourself. If you make widgets, what makes your widgets better than anyone else's? If you perform a service, how do you do it faster or more effectively? Your branding is what sets you apart!

Let's assume you are a real estate agent. This shouldn't be much of a stretch for most readers. If you brand yourself as "Sally Smith, REALTOR," how exactly does that set you apart? Think about how many other agents are in your city. Even in small towns, the number can be extreme. If I am scrolling down my news feed on Facebook, that name is not going to stand out. Now, something snazzy like, "Sally Smith, Real Estate Superstar" might grab my attention. The problem is that it still doesn't really tell me what sets you apart, only that you have an ego. Perhaps something along the lines of "Sally Smith, Dream Home Finder" or "Sally Smith, Waterfront Wizard," would paint a more captivating portrait.

Whatever you decide you want your brand to be, sell it! Let every post be a testament to your abilities, knowledge, and passion. Make people believe you are the expert in your field, and all others are amateurs, at best! By selecting the right content and consistently promoting yourself, you can build a recognizable brand for little or no capital investment. There is no shortage of content to support whichever niche you choose. You just have find it and use it.

Be a Resource

It's no secret that providing information or a service will help endear you to a potential customer. People are eager to find benefit in a business partnership. They want to know that you have value and that you aren't just trying to "close the deal." Give them something of value and they will almost feel obligated to at least give you the time of day.

Let's assume Sally decided on "Waterfront Wizard" as her brand. Simply saying she is an expert doesn't make it so. She has to establish a track record. At the very least, this can be accomplished through the right content. She at least LOOKS like an expert. However, to move the customer out of the "friend zone" of the relationship, she may need to provide some value. She could research upcoming events at the local marina or find out where the best fishing spots are. Those are just two of the many ideas that an agent could use to be a resource. You want convey the message, "I understand what is important to you."

Providing value to your customers creates a bond. It's a bond that, over time, can be cultivated into a possible sale or even a stream of referral business. Don't look at every person you encounter as a sale to close. Try to learn what makes them tick and sell yourself to that part of them. You are not selling your service; you are selling you! Make sure they see your true value.

Top-of-Mind Awareness

Let's face it. Technology has made people extremely forgetful. I have hundreds of Facebook friends that I can't even remember how I know them or why I accepted their friend request. Don't even get me started on LinkedIn connections. I have over 1,600 of those! The drawback is that it is hard enough to differentiate yourself. Getting people to constantly re-remember you is another challenge all together. I heard a statistic at my first National Association of REALTORS convention in 2001, and it has stuck with me. People will forget you after an average of 17 days! Obviously, this is not applicable to close friends or even some acquaintances. Stay in sales long enough, though, and you will experience the pain of the words, "I forgot you sold X." It is not a great feeling.

Social media has made it so incredibly easy to increase top-of-mind awareness. Some people think the sun rises and sets by their social media news feed. All you need to do is be consistent. Websites like Facebook work on mathematic principles that decide what people see and at what frequency. It rewards consistency and engagement. This means all you need to do is post the right content at the right intervals, and your name will keep appearing in front of your target audience.

Awareness is essential for your survival and cannot be overlooked. We will look at methods to increase your exposure to maximize not only the number of people who see you, but the frequency at which you appear. If you play your cards right, being forgotten could be a thing of the past!!

Have Fun

Just because you are using it for business doesn't mean social media can't be fun too. In fact, fun is an essential component. I have a blast on Instagram, and my followers see that. The more fun I have, the more engaged my fans are. Social media marketing should never be a chore. An element of fun should be included in every marketing plan you create.

If you aren't having fun, people will see right through you. They will probably think you are boring, and no one wants to do business with a stick in the mud. Let your personality shine through. If you love cooking, share recipes or videos of you making something tasty. Maybe you love the torture of running marathons. Other people (not myself) may find that entertaining. For the record, if my body is ever discovered on a jogging trail, please know that I was killed somewhere else and dumped there. I digress. The point is, people like working with people like them. Finding common ground through shared interests is a great way to build rapport. Social media is the perfect outlet to spread the word about your hobbies.

Chapter 2: You're Doing It Wrong!

As with almost everything in life, there is a wrong way to do social media. In fact, if you aren't careful, your social media habits could start costing you business. In this chapter, I am going to focus on some of the activities and topics that tend to be major pitfalls for social media users. If you are guilty of any of these offenses, don't beat yourself up. We have ALL made these mistakes at one time or another. The important thing is that you commit to walking the right path from this point forward.

Repetitive Posting

This tends to be the go-to method for folks that lack the confidence in their own creativity. Instead of searching for new and interesting things to talk about, they stick with what they think has worked in the past. There is also a small minority that does this because they either don't know or don't care what it is that will engage their followers. As we will discuss later, you have to know your audience! Here are some examples of repetitive postings we have all seen at one point or another:

"Call me if you need to buy or sell."

"Check out my new listing."

"Don't forget, I sell real estate."

"Check out my listing." <For the 5th time in 7 days>

You might be saying to yourself, "Well, you just told me I have to stay top-of-mind. How else can I do that if I don't tell people I'm in real estate?" I'm glad you asked! There was one crucial element missing from all the above posts – Value! There was nothing offered to the reader that would entice them to engage, let alone to want your services. Content is king in social media. Simply telling people about yourself isn't going to cut it anymore. What is in it for them? I'll give you some pointers later about ways to gently remind people that you sell homes, but in an engaging manner

Bragging

Now don't get all up in arms. I'm not saying that a little self-promotion is a bad thing. In fact, you can't survive in business without it. Unfortunately, most salespeople feel that the more they brag about how much they have sold; the more people will flock to them. That's simply not the case in most situations anymore. As a millennial, I can tell you that my generation, in particular, doesn't care how great you think you are. We want to know what is in it for us! We will likely tune you completely out on social media if that's all we see. If that happens, how will you ever get our business?

Apart from people ignoring you, I have seen bragging backfire in several costly ways. The first example is an all too familiar one concerning commissions. Bill just had the best year of his career and has been talking non-stop on social media about being a multi-million-dollar producer. He gets a listing appointment and lays out an incredible marketing plan. He feels confident! Right as he is getting ready to close the deal, the seller asks if he will cut his commission. Bill cannot figure out where he went wrong. Little does he know, the seller thinks "multi-million-dollar producer" means Bill is a millionaire. Certainly, Bill can afford a few thousand dollars off his fee! The sad truth is that the public, by and large, does not understand the intricacies of the real estate industry. They don't know how hard agents work because we only talk about the successes. This seller didn't have an appreciation for the value Bill was bringing to the table. All Bill ever talks about is how successful he is.

The second dangerous bragging scenario happened before my very eyes. Starting in 2013, Nashville, TN, experienced a lightning-fast shift into a sellers' market. Homes were literally flying off the shelves. Many agents were experiencing immense success. That's when the danger began to occur. All over social media were stories of homes that were listed at 9:00 AM and under contract by noon for $20,000 over list price with 7 offers. It was a very exciting time! However, I made a prediction that began to come true. I remember saying to an agent, "Pretty soon, sellers are going to catch on to this trend and start asking why they even need an agent." Within a few weeks, For Sale by Owner signs were becoming a common sight. It made perfect sense. As a seller, why would I give away $15,000 of MY money to someone who will only be doing about 4 hours of work? It sounds like I can just slap a sign in my yard and cash in (That's certainly what I did!).

Agents get so caught up in the excitement of success that they forget that public perception is vitally important to that success. When I started my career, long before Facebook and Twitter, I was taught never to say "I'm busy." I was taught to say, "I could always be busier" or "I always have time for more clients." To say I was busy, was taken as "I don't have time for you." Agents do that all the time on social media and don't even realize it. Be more conscious of how you present yourself and the market to the public. Make sure you are painting the right portrait.

Politics and Religion

I have no doubt that some of you rolled your eyes and some nodded in agreement. I apologize in advance, but this topic gets a little touchy for many people. However, it's something that must be addressed. Delving into these topics on social media is a dangerous move for your business. You can risk alienating large groups of potential clients with a single post.

As I write this, the 2016 Presidential Election has social media abuzz over the results. No matter what side you were on, we can probably all agree that this was an historic election. I can say that this was the worst campaign I have ever witnessed, in terms of division. Everyone still has very strong opinions, and the wound is still raw.

What exactly do your political opinions have to do with your job? Unless you are actually in politics, nothing whatever! Your personal beliefs on how this country should be run has zero bearing on how you sell a house, a car, or a widget. I consider myself to be pretty thick-skinned and am not easily offended. However, I will admit that my opinions of some people changed. It wasn't that they disagreed with my beliefs, it was the way in which it was done. I have never seen so much disdain and vitriol on social media as I did leading up to November 8, 2016. If I felt that way, think how a customer or client felt.

Too often (I am guilty of this as well), we assume that people think like us. Therefore, whatever we say should be accepted and agreed upon. It's absolutely not the case! The sad part is that you may never know that you lost that $500,000 sale. That customer was going to call you until you posted that last nasty comment. They simply called someone else. Ask yourself if voicing your opinion that will make no difference in the grand scheme of things is worth losing major money. It certainly isn't in my book. Maybe you can afford to lose money, but many people cannot.

Religion is the other hot button issue. In my opinion, religion can be a bigger danger than politics because of its constancy. Politics only gets really heated every 2 years or so with minor flare ups here and there. Religion is an everyday thing for many people. The same concepts hold true with religion as with politics. Your beliefs don't really have any impact on your job function and don't assume people agree with you. This is a free country and you have the ability to hold or reject whatever beliefs you wish. Just be careful when talking about it on social media.

If you want to be really cautious, don't talk about it at all! I know that sounds a bit much for some people.

Sharing your faith may be a strong conviction you hold. If you feel so inclined, be sure you always do so respectfully. There is no need to bash a different faith or even a denomination of your own faith to get your point across.

Here is a thought experiment. Say, a buyer walks into your office with a proof of funds letter for $1 million cash, and they need to find a house in the next 3 days. As you drive them around, the conversation gets personal. For some reason, you reveal that you are a Catholic (This is just an example. Don't freak out on me). Then they mention they are a Baptist. Do you slam on the brakes and throw them out of your car? It's highly unlikely. What if they are Muslim or Jewish or even Atheist? I am willing to bet that you can set aside your opinions for this deal to go through. If you agree that the transaction would continue unabated, great! Here's the thing. When you say negative things about other faiths on social media, you are essentially throwing them out of your car. If you show intolerance toward their beliefs, why would they want to work with you?

My whole point is very simple. If you don't mind limiting your client pool by potentially half, then by all means, share your opinions openly. Personally, I like making money, and if my opinion will cost me, I keep it to myself. There is nothing wrong with engaging in friendly banter or sharing a personal story. However, be sure to check your tone. Step outside of the situation and ask if this could be misconstrued. Better yet, ask yourself, "Could this cost me business?" If the answer is yes, post something else.

Stalking Customers

When you think stalking, you probably see visions of sneaking around someone's house or digging through trash to find nail clippings. Business stalking is much more civilized but still fairly annoying. I am only going to touch on a few behaviors in this section, but it should be enough so you get the gist.

3-Year-Old Photos

You are so excited! The owner of that huge mansion just accepted your friend request after you met at that mixer! Oh, if only you could get in good with her. She probably has lots of rich friends she could refer to you!! You better let her know that you think she's great. The best thing you can do is to go back in her photo album and spend 45 minutes liking and commenting on her old pictures.

Sound familiar? We have all had that one friend that likes photos from yesteryear. It might seem nice at first. However, when you stop to think about how long it takes to scroll back that far in your album, it kind of starts to feel creepy. Don't be like that. Only like and comment on current events. Don't be a photo creeper.

First Like or Comment, Every Time

Next, we have the folks that always seem to be the first to like and comment on EVERY post you make. Again, at first it seems cute. Pretty soon you start to wonder if they are literally sitting there waiting for you to say something. It's best to keep a little distance from customers and clients. A couple of touches per week is good. Every day gets to be a little much.

Bulk Attention

I have to give a shout out to my friend and colleague Mary V. She is the only person that has the ability to make me want to like 15 posts at once. She is well known for her hilarious memes on Facebook. I find myself scrolling down my news feed liking 10-12 posts of hers before I even realize what I've done. It's a good thing I've already had this discussion with her, or she may think I am a little unstable. In this case, I have a pass. However, in the course of normal business, you may want to avoid what I call "bulk attention." Throughout the day, liking and sharing 2-3 posts is acceptable. More than 5 and I start to wonder. Remember, everything in moderation.

LinkedIn "Over" View

I love it when people view my profile on LinkedIn! I have worked very hard on it, and I want it to be seen. You can find a link in the Appendix. However, there comes a point when viewing someone's profile every other day gets creepy. LinkedIn profiles are not that dynamic, meaning they don't change often. There is no reason you should be on there unless I have had an update. Trust me on this, people notice. It's not just me!

There are so many other ways not to accomplish your social media goals. These are just a few of my favorites. If you ever wonder if you're making a mistake, just ask yourself, "Do I like it when people do this to me?" If the answer is no, then you can probably figure out that you shouldn't do it. A big part of marketing is just common sense. The same holds true for social media.

Chapter 3: The 5 C's

I know. "It's about time!" I had to lay down some context first before diving into the good stuff. As I said, the 5 C's are basically the distilled version of my social media philosophy. I have tapped into my years of social media marketing experience, coaching, and training to create a simple list of easy-to-grasp concepts. These work for me and have worked for many others. I hope you find them beneficial.

Connection

This one almost goes without saying … almost. Believe it or not, there are people out there that don't realize that failing to connect with people on social media doesn't help their efforts. Connection actually has a double meaning. The first is the obvious one. You need friends, fans, followers, and likes. The second meaning is "a deeper." Literally, I mean a deeper connection. Finding a way to really connect with people on a personal level can increase your effectiveness several times over. Let's look at both more in depth.

Getting the Word Out

Failing to promote your social media profile is the biggest mistake you can make. People aren't just going to magically come to you. I have had a business page for over 3 years, and I just recently hit the 500 likes mark. It was a proud moment for me because my likes are all organic. By that, I mean that I didn't pay for artificial recognition. Share your profiles on all your marketing and cross-promote on other outlets. Give people a reason to want to be connected (content). The more you talk about it, the more people will begin to listen.

Some other mistakes I see accompany this issue. One that drives me nuts is the secretive folks. They either have their privacy settings set extremely high, don't have a photo, or are using their middle name as their last name. That last one is especially perplexing on LinkedIn, since there is little or nothing people can do to you even if they figure out who you are. Stop being so paranoid! How can people connect with you if they can't even find you? If you are that worried about someone stalking or messing with you, just get off social media. You aren't accomplishing anything anyway.

Get a Little Personal

I'm not saying you have to share your life story on social media. In fact, there is quite a bit you should keep to yourself. However, it doesn't hurt to make an attempt to connect with people on a more personal level. Talk about what you love. Someone else probably loves it too! Are you funny (not funny looking)? Then let your sense of humor shine through. Just be sure to keep it appropriate for the audience. No matter what the angle is, try to go just a bit deeper with people. You may be amazed at the results.

Content

You have officially arrived. This is the mother lode! In the world of social media marketing, content is king. Content is what engages your followers, increases your reach, and puts your name in front of people you've never even met. It is the engine that drives your marketing machine. Unfortunately, it's also the one thing most people ignore when building their plans. Promoting your social media presence without content is like trying to propel a boat with a spatula. You may get somewhere, but it probably won't be where you want and you'll eventually just give up.

Likeable and Shareable

If there are two words you need to remember from this book, they are "likeable" and "shareable." Your all-consuming goal for social media posts should be to meet those criteria. Those words should be a litmus test for every post you create. As I said before, you want people to pass your post on because attached to it is your name. What is the #1 goal of social media again? Name Recognition! Whenever you create a post, I want you to ask one very important question, "Who cares?" I mean that in the most literal way possible. If you can't identify anyone that would actually care about the content of the post, it's fairly useless. To be clear, I am referring to business posts, not personal. It needs to be something that someone will like or share. It's as simple as that.

Content Creation

For the really savvy folks out there, you can create your own content and customize it to your needs and audience. An example would be a blog. The content is original, unique, and written from your personal perspective, a trait many people find appealing. If you are REALLY into it, you could create infographics. They are very popular on social media. The issue with content creation is, of course, time. We are busy sales professionals. Who has hours to set aside for blogging or even researching the post material? The other obstacle is creativity. Let's face it. Not everyone is cut from that cloth. There is nothing wrong with that. Even the most creative people struggle occasionally with topic creation. Content creation is not for everyone. If you are good at it, bravo!

Content Syndication

Just because you don't have the time or desire to create your own content, doesn't mean you can't have one of the best social media campaigns out there. There is SO much amazing content out there for the taking. Content creators LOVE it when people re-post their work. Just be sure to always link back to the original source. You are not stealing their work. You are syndicating it. People don't really care who wrote a piece of information, but they are more likely to remember who brought it to their attention. Wouldn't it be great if that person was you?

Oh, and in case you are wondering, I am mostly a syndicator. I do have a blog and, of course, I write books. However, I am a busy person too! I find it much easier to simply re-distribute great content already created and proven effective. It works well for me.

The Breakdown

Now it's time to choose your content. This is the hardest part for most people. Some choose topics that are too general or too specific. Some only talk about business. Some never talk about business. Striking a balance is key. Here is one theory to which I subscribe.

50% Entertaining or Engaging

Half of what you post should simply be focused on grabbing the customer's attention. This can be accomplished by something purely entertaining or something targeted to the customer's specific interests. Either way, it's likeable and shareable and gets your name out there!

40% Helpful or Informative

This is where the value comes in. You have gotten their attention by being entertaining. Now you can reel them in by offering help or knowledge. This is particularly important in niche marketing. Imagine you are trying to carve out that waterfront niche. Simply telling people you are an expert doesn't go very far. You can increase engagement by targeting your content to people who either own or want to own waterfront property. Remember, you are selling the perception of

"I understand you." Perhaps you post an article titled, "5 Easy Steps to Winterizing Your Boat" or "15 Family-friendly Water Games." Now you have found something that might interest them.

10% Product or Service

Notice how the heading says, "10%?" I'm glad you see it! It really should say, "No More Than 10%." Unfortunately, many people out there talk about their product or service 90% of the time. That is no way to engage an audience. When I worked for American Home Shield, the country's largest home warranty provider, my job was to convince real estate agents to recommend my product. I used social media as an integral part of my business plan. Do you know how often I actually posted anything about home warranties? MAYBE once a month. It was normally like once a quarter.

I was the first to admit that home warranties are not the most interesting topic in the world. It wasn't easy to captivate my readers with content about a specific product. I focused on what engaged my audience, and it worked! I achieved great name recognition and actually branded myself as a social media marketing expert. Agents who had never worked with me before would call me for advice on their marketing. That eventually led to us doing business together. I provided a value, and the relationship took root.

Naturally, you need to talk about what you do. However, there are much subtler ways to accomplish this. I will discuss these more in depth as I break down the various platforms. The rule of thumb to remember is, if you must post solely about your product or service, try to limit it to once a week. That's a nice, safe place to be.

Don't Freak Out!

The hardest part of social media marketing is actually DOING it! I hear the same reasons over and over again: "I'm too busy," "I don't know how," "I'm not that creative," and "I don't think it will work for my market." The list goes on. Some people just need a little jolt of motivation to get them going. I hope this book can help provide that. Others need a guiding hand, someone to coach them toward good behaviors and show how all the dots connect.

I am sure there are still some of you that are thinking, *"I could never do all that!"* It's nowhere near as difficult as it sounds. It just takes practice and a little commitment. There is good news for those of you who are still unsure. **You can hire someone to do it for you!** I don't mean get an assistant. Unless you already have one, in which case, get him or her to do it. There are companies out there that will take the bulk of the marketing headache off your plate. A simple search will yield hundreds of companies willing to take on the responsibility. Just **DO YOUR RESEARCH!** There are plenty of bad apples out there!

No matter what you do, focus on your content! It will single-handedly make or break your marketing campaign. Content is also the only of the 5 C's that will accomplish all the purposes of social media laid out earlier. You could almost say that it is THE C of social media, because without content, everything else is useless.

Consistency

I have seen some agents that have 1,500 or more friends and even some halfway decent content fail miserably at social media marketing because they can't maintain a consistent presence. They don't understand the underlying mathematics that drive social media sites, so their brilliant posts fall on deaf ears. You don't have to make that same mistake.

The Mechanics

I don't claim to fully understand how every social media site works. I am not a super computer. These sites are built on extremely complex mathematical algorithms that dictate their behavior and are constantly changing. I do know enough, however, to shed a glimmer of light on how things are connected.

Let's look at Facebook. I'm sure you've noticed by now that despite the fact that you have hundreds or even thousands of friends, you only see posts from maybe 50 people in any given day. Because of this, I completely forget that I am even friends with people! The reason behind this limitation is your engagement. Facebook looks at the people with whom you interact and the frequency. From there, it determines whose posts you see and how often. This comprises your news feed. Are you with me so far?

Business pages are even more limited than your personal news feed. Facebook gives a much lower priority to pages than profiles. This is partly because if you saw every post from every page you like, your news feed would be overrun. Mostly, at least in my opinion, it's because Facebook wants to charge you for "Boosting" your post. Maybe I am just being cynical, but it makes sense. The end result is that unless you CONSTANTLY stay connected with people, you will literally vanish from their news feed. Maybe Scooby and the Gang can help solve the mystery of where you went.

The Solution

Consistency is the most effective solution to the mystery of the disappearing friend. Thankfully, Facebook doesn't require daily interaction, at least not yet. For Business Pages, I recommend at least one post a day, Monday – Friday. That's a minimum of 5 posts a week. It's really not all that much. However, you have to also make time to actually create or find the content before you can post it. Even so, it's a small price to pay to stay in front of your target audience. Another solution is to simply pay money to "Boost" the post. That gets expensive very quickly.

The Pitfalls

Most people I know set out on their social media journey with the best of intentions but quickly stray from the path. Even I was guilty of this in the beginning. Weeks one and two go well. You get likes, and your posts are well received. Then week three rolls around, and you get busy. Maybe you only manage 3 posts. Week four, you only post twice. By now, Facebook has caught on and has already started removing you from view of others. Pretty soon, you are lucky to get a single like on your weekly post about your newest listings. It's a vicious cycle. The numbers drop, so you lose motivation and slacken your content quality. That leads to even less engagement, which decreases motivation even more. In the end, social media is just another place for you to post properties. The sad truth is that it doesn't take long to derail your progress. Facebook is like a toddler. If you turn your back, you may not like the consequences.

Not All Doom and Gloom

Have I sufficiently scared you? It was not my intention. However, I would not be doing my job if I sugar-coated this issue. You can't fight the algorithm. As I said before, it just takes a little commitment to succeed. Don't waste the time finding or creating content if you can't manage to post consistently. Once you get into the groove, your social media campaigns shouldn't take you much more than 30-45 minutes a week to set up and schedule. Again, an assistant or a company can completely take that burden off your shoulders. Any way you choose to do it, just be sure to be consistent!

Cohesion

This is probably the most difficult concept to grasp, but it is still critically important to your overall branding success. You can accomplish your goals without cohesion, but it will vastly improve your focus and effectiveness on social media. Having a unified message also adds credibility and lessens any confusion on the part of the consumer.

Niche + Cohesion = Branding

I can hear it already, "What on Earth is 'cohesion'?" To put it simply, cohesion is the unification of your message. I'll start at the beginning. I think everyone should have at least 2 specialties in their marketing. For instance, niche #1 could be "Millennials" and niche #2 could be "Urban Living." Those are 2 beautifully complementary niches since Millennials are far more likely to desire an urban setting for their home purchase. Cohesion comes in when you choose your content. If you are marketing yourself as an urban expert, don't post things regarding equestrian properties. It will take away from your core message. What if Starbucks introduced a line of steaks? That is completely outside of their wheelhouse. Frankly, it would only confuse their loyal customer base and would likely fail utterly. Cohesion is choosing content that strengthens the image you project.

Not only do you need cohesion between your message and your niches, you need it within your chosen niches. You should not desire to be all things to all customers.

In this scenario, niche #1 is "First-Time Homebuyers" and niche #2 is "Vacation Homes." Seriously?? Those two things couldn't be further apart! Unless you want to run two completely separate campaigns, these niches will conflict. It will be nearly impossible to find content that can marry these concepts.

In order to build a strong personal brand, you need to specialize and differentiate. Find specialties that match your skillset and passion. If you truly love what you do, people will be drawn to you. Passion is contagious. Once you select your niches, commit to finding content that supports and showcases them. Everything you post should tie into your brand. You are the expert, and your content will back you up.

Cross-platform Cohesion

Now that you have chosen complementary niches and content to enhance them, it's time to look at the bigger picture. You have to be sure that you have cohesion across all the social media platforms you utilize. It's not wise to have one niche on Facebook, another on LinkedIn, and a third on Pinterest, and something completely different on Instagram. It's very likely that many of your connections span across some or all of your accounts. Just as before, a fractured message only creates confusion. You said on Facebook that your passion was "First-time Homebuyers," but then all you post on Instagram are pictures of million-dollar mansions. It is simply not an effective way to market yourself. If you choose multiple platforms, be sure to focus on a unified message.

I have a two-pronged approach in my marketing. My niche is simple, "I help agents and companies be more successful." Therefore, my content is chosen to reflect that. My first type of post is information that will directly help my reader. It could be social media tips, negotiating tactics, or whatever I think is useful. The second type is consumer-facing content they can share in their marketing efforts. I am a strong believer in social media marketing, obviously. I want to encourage agents that follow my content to create a strong market for themselves. Anything I can do to accomplish that, achieves my purpose. That's cohesion!

Communication

Much like connections, this C almost goes without saying. Since I already brought it up, I'll go ahead and say it anyway. You must communicate with your audience! The content is just there to grab their attention. Once they engage with you, reciprocation is absolutely necessary. If someone comments on a post, the very least you can do is like the comment. Let them know that you noticed. Social media engagement is a two-way street. The best way to connect with your audience is to communicate. Don't just talk AT them. Talk TO them.

You also need to be prepared for the possibility that folks will use messaging features of social media to initiate contact. When I worked for American Home Shield, I had several agents that would order all their warranties with me via Facebook Messenger. At the very least, you should familiarize yourself with the technology enough to respond. You can always move the conversation off-line later.

So there you have the 5 C's of Social Media of Social Media Success. Are you completely overwhelmed? If so, you are not alone. Many people have an adverse reaction when confronted with information that challenges preconceived notions. Now that we have discussed theory, let's delve into some practical applications. We will start by first understanding some of the features of the various platforms and how you can apply what you've learned in each.

Chapter 4: Applying the Theory

The 5 C's give you a broad understanding of how best to accomplish your social media goals. The real challenge is knowing how they fit in each platform. Many social media sites share basic similarities while some are wildly variant in their correct usage and target audience. In this chapter, we will examine several of the more popular platforms and how you can best apply what you have learned so far in order to maximize your effectiveness.

Facebook

I will start at the obvious. Facebook is, by far, the largest social media site in the world with just under 1.8 billion users worldwide. Being the largest has allowed Facebook to basically set the "gold standard" when it comes to social media interaction. Despite its size, or perhaps because of it, Facebook is not always on the cutting edge. You may notice newer features like live video and the Marketplace. These are recent additions to the arsenal of tools, but are by no means original ideas. Facebook adapts and moves with the trends it sees in its users. We too must pay attention to the trends and adjust our strategy accordingly.

Know Your Audience

When Facebook started, it was by and large a young crowd. People in their late teens and mid-twenties abandoned MySpace with staggering speed. It was "cool" to have a Facebook page. As time progressed, older generations began to see benefits in having a profile. Today, the Baby Boomers make a large segment of the American Facebook populace. Meanwhile, my younger cousins in their mid-teens see it as "lame" to be on Facebook with all the old folks. They also view e-mail like we now see faxing, but that's another conversation entirely. The point is that Millennials are probably the last generation to have any major presence on this platform. Don't lose hope, that still leaves millions of potential customers to farm. The other thing to remember is that most of the kids who think it's lame don't really have the financial ability to make a major purchase anyway. It's a win-win, for now.

Business vs. Personal

I'll admit that I get sucked into all the nonsense my friends get up to. If I'm not careful, I can waste an hour just scrolling down my news feed. On the personal side, I am a certified junkie! However, I am a firm believer in keeping a separation between your personal and professional lives. That applies to all areas of my life, not just social media. Thankfully, Facebook has created Business Pages for just that purpose. The main difference between the two is the that personal profiles get "friends," while Business Pages get "likes." A like on a page basically tells the almighty algorithm that you are interested in posts from that company. As we learned earlier, it doesn't take long for your page to vanish from their view if there is no engagement.

If you don't have a Business Page, get one! Just do it already. There is nothing to be afraid of. You can't properly brand yourself or track your effectiveness with just a personal profile. If you don't know how, there are plenty of tutorials that can help. There are also companies out there that can build you one for a fee. Personally, if I didn't want to do it myself, I would go to Fiverr and pay someone on there to do it. Fiverr (www.fiverr.com) is a website where you can engage the services of individuals for a multitude of online tasks. You can easily find someone to help you out with page creation. I'd do it for you, but I'm super busy liking Mary's cat memes.

Judging Your Effectiveness

Let me just start off by saying that I am, by no means, an authority on the subject of Facebook metrics. If you have a better understanding or a better way of accomplishing this, I salute you. In fact, feel free to share your insights with me. As with everything in this book, I am simply sharing my experience and what has worked for me and others to whom I have spoken.

Likes

There are several ways to track your success on a Facebook Business Page. The first one is obviously page likes. You have to get people to like the page in order for your content to reach them. Once they like the page, they are considered a "fan." This is accomplished by good, old fashioned marketing. Tell people about it in all your marketing and ask them to like your page. I don't recommend paying for a service or even boosting your page unless you have an extremely targeted audience. These likes are usually fairly useless and will probably never transact with you. "But Stephen, you said it was all about name recognition." That's true, but who cares if someone in St. Petersburg, Russia, knows you're in real estate. I doubt they are buying in America anytime soon. It's best to focus on organic growth. Find people that might actually generate some business someday.

Post likes are another way to measure your effectiveness. I use it to get a quick glimpse of how well my content was received. If I get multiple likes, it tells me that I picked a topic that is of interest to people. I use it as positive reinforcement. No likes received could be telling me I didn't strike a nerve or posted at a bad time. Timing can play an important role in this as well. These are the simplest ways to quickly assess your activities.

Reach

There are actually several kinds of reach to discuss. I'll try to break them down as easily as possible.

- Total Reach – This number represents the number of people who "saw" your post, including paid and organic.
- Organic Reach – This is the number of people who saw the post not resulting from any action (paid boost, liking, sharing, etc …).
- Viral Reach – These are the resulting views generated from a friend sharing or liking the post and it being seen by someone else on their news feed.

For my purposes, I like to track my reach. Since I never pay for boosting, I don't have skewed numbers. I want to know what people REALLY want to see. Viral reach is my favorite because that tells me my content is shareable and that makes me happy!

Engagement

This is fairly straightforward. Engagement is anyone who clicked anywhere on the post. They didn't just see it; they took an action. This can include: liking, reacting, commenting, sharing, or watching a video. This is when you know you have really hit on a great subject. Your goal should always be to increase engagement.

There are many more complex ways you can track your effectiveness like: click-through rate, people talking about this, or even negative feedback. In all honesty, the three I touched on are the only ones I have found vital to my purposes. You could spend hours analyzing the data and fine-tuning your results. At the end of the day, it comes down to intuition. If one post did better than another post, maybe you should do more on that subject. If you notice your number dropping, do some research on timing. Otherwise, focus on finding amazing content that will leave your audience wanting more!

LinkedIn

I think LinkedIn is one of the most underestimated and underutilized platforms for real estate agents. Most people view LinkedIn as simply an online version of their résumé. While it does serve that purpose, there is so much more to it! LinkedIn is a professional networking site where members can showcase their business acumen through several effective methods. LinkedIn does share some similar features to Facebook but is unique in many ways.

Business vs. Personal

If I am being honest, there should be no personal side to LinkedIn. It's strictly a professional site. In fact, some members will comment if people post political, religious, overly personal, or inflammatory content on the site. The LinkedIn mantra tends to be, "This isn't Facebook!" Your goal here is to build business, not to share funny animal memes and crude jokes. Another main difference between LinkedIn and Facebook is the terminology. On Facebook, you have friends. On LinkedIn, you have connections.

Because LinkedIn is strictly business, it's much less distracting. I find that I only need a fraction of the time to take care of my business on LinkedIn as opposed to Facebook. This is due to the fact that I spend about an hour mindlessly scrolling down my news feed. You won't be (or at least you shouldn't) posting every 45 minutes about where you are, who you've seen, or what you are eating. It's actually quite liberating once you get used to it.

LinkedIn *Dos* and *Don'ts*

These are not hard and fast rules for LinkedIn success. Again, these are just best practices that I have picked up over the years. They are also suggestions to keep you out of the cross-hairs of picky members. The LinkedIn community likes to police itself, and those who stray from the path tend to be ridiculed, even if it's just a little jab here and there.

Do – Complete Your Profile

Have you changed jobs recently? Did you get another degree or certification? Make sure you include this kind of information on your profile. It's pretty pathetic when I get a notification telling me you have a work anniversary when I know you left that company 6 months ago. I put every stitch of experience on my profile from when I started my real estate career in 2001. You just never know what might be relevant. You also need a good tag line. When I worked for American Home Shield, my job title was Account Executive. However, my tag line said, "Results-oriented Sales Trainer/Author/Coach." That's a lot more impressive and indicative of what my talents are. Be sure to sell yourself in your profile!

For the love of all that is holy, PLEASE make sure your contact information is correct! This rule applies to ALL forms of social media. Most smart phones allow data from social media to sync with your contacts. If your profile is incorrect, how will people get in touch with you? I get so frustrated when I want to call or e-mail someone from my smart phone, and their information is either missing or incorrect. It could be that you just lost a sale because I couldn't reach you.

My other pet peeve is when people don't have photos. I am a visual person. I like to be able to match faces and names. Many times, I won't add someone on LinkedIn who has no picture. In my mind, they either don't care or don't use the site enough to be of any use to me. When you DO upload a photo, it better not be a glamour shot or your high school yearbook photo from 1976. You may not like your current appearance, but that is how people will recognize you.

Don't – Use an Unrecognizable Name

I am sure some of you looked at this and thought, "What in the world is he talking about?" I am sure you have seen people on Facebook that use their middle name instead of their last name so people can't easily find them. Well, believe it or not, there are folks that do it on LinkedIn too! There is no conceivable reason any sane person can concoct that would justify making yourself hard to find on a networking site. Let that last part sink in for a minute. If you are that scared, call the cops. The fact is, there is pretty much nothing anyone can DO to you on LinkedIn. They can't post on your wall like on Facebook. The entire point is to connect with people. Don't make it harder than it already is.

Do – Accept Connections

Again, unlike Facebook, it's pretty safe to accept connections from pretty much anyone. So what if he's a Nigerian prince? He can't do anything to you, and it might look good to have a royal connection. The point of networking is to build your sphere of influence. How is that going to be accomplished if you only connect with the people you know. I'm not advocating spamming everyone in your city. LinkedIn doesn't allow that anyway. You just never know when a random connection might come in handy someday.

Don't – Ignore Messages and Comments

This is one of those areas where the way you interact on LinkedIn and Facebook are pretty similar. If people comment on your posts and articles or send you private messages, RESPOND! At the very least, acknowledge that you've seen it. As a general rule, ignoring things like that on social media is considered rude. LinkedIn is no different. If you can't commit to logging in daily, just get the app on your phone and look for notifications. It seriously takes less than 30 seconds to respond.

Do – Create a Niche

LinkedIn is a great place to hone your niche. The business world is even more content-sensitive than consumers. If you want to add value, the posts better be good. Show your stuff by choosing or writing content that supports your marketing plan. I am not going to beat a dead horse on this subject. Just don't underestimate the power of a good niche on LinkedIn.

Do – Endorse and Recommend

Try to get into the habit of spending a little time every day on LinkedIn. The more you interact with others, the more they will reciprocate. Endorsements are the easiest way to help out a connection. You select what skills you wish to promote on your profile. Then LinkedIn makes suggestions to your connections to endorse you. For instance, you might see, "Does Stephen Know About 'Coaching'?" Then all you have to do is click the "Endorse" button, and it is added to their profile. People are then able to see how many endorsements that person has for a particular skill.

Recommendations are even more powerful! It is basically a review of that person. You can select a person and tell LinkedIn for which position you are writing the recommendation and your relationship to that person within the confines of that position. Then, it is as simple as just writing a paragraph or two about how great that person is. They can even ask for revisions, if they like. It's an incredible way to help out a business colleague. Here is my one piece of advice that you all need to hear. When someone writes you a recommendation, WRITE ONE BACK IN RETURN!!!! It's the very least you can do. If you ever get a recommendation from me, I expect one back, just so you know.

The Art of Posting

Next, I want to explore and explain the 2 main ways that you can share content on LinkedIn. They are both useful, but one has more staying power over the other. Content plays an even more important role on LinkedIn, so that should be your focus. Once you have your material chosen, you can find the best place to put it.

Share an Update

This one is very simple. LinkedIn has a news feed, much like Facebook. Content hits the feed and within hours, it has disappeared from sight. Getting maximum exposure requires proper timing. For the record, posting between 7:00 A.M. and 9:00 A.M. is what most of the research I have seen suggests. Business people don't spend endless hours throughout the day trolling LinkedIn to see what their friends had for lunch. It's an activity that's done in the morning while drinking coffee or on the subway commuting to work. Updates should be attention grabbing. The goal is to attract enough interest so the reader sees you name and tag line. It's really as simple as that, if they click on the post, so much the better.

Write an Article

This used to be called "Publish a Post," but even I thought that was confusing. Many people would assume a post was an update, like on Facebook. The new moniker is much less confusing. An article is much like a blog on your profile. The beauty part is that articles stay on your profile to show how prolific you are with your content. The library of articles has incredible staying power and lends credibility to your niche.

As with all content, you can either be a Generator or Syndicator on LinkedIn. Original content is, of course, the most desirable. However, time constraints being what they are, it's not always easy to consistently create new material. Here is what I do. I find a great article on a topic that aligns with my niche. I copy and paste the body of the article, and sometimes the photo. At the beginning, I write a **BOLD-format** paragraph about why I chose to feature this article. Sometimes, I even mention the author by name. Then at the bottom, I paste the original source URL. You might think this seems like cheating or plagiarizing. I disagree. I never mislead people to think I am the author, and I ALWAYS provide a link to the source. This actually helps the author by driving more traffic to the original site. That's the power of syndication and why people generate content to start with. I do generate a fair amount of my own material, but I am not an expert on every topic. I see nothing wrong with reaching outside myself to find great content to help my followers learn new skills.

Instagram

For those of you who don't like to write, you're in luck. As the old saying goes, "A picture's worth a thousand words." Instagram is a photo and video posting platform owned by Facebook. It's primarily accessed on a smart phone or tablet. I get questions all the time about using Instagram for business purposes, which are to encourage engagement and add value. It's hard to grasp how posting photos can add value for a customer. I completely understand and will endeavor to explain.

Instagram Engagement

This is almost a no-brainer. People love photos! They love all kinds like: interesting, emotional, cute, funny, wild, crazy, even gross. Taking and posting photos is the easy part. The skill comes when it's time to connect it with business. Subtlety is the key to success. When you can learn to drop little hints while engaging your fan base, you will see a noticeable increase in your name recognition and hopefully, web traffic to other profiles.

Audience Polls

One of the easiest ways to get engagement from followers is to ask their opinion. People love to tell you what they think! Here is an example of an engaging audience poll that also uses subtle messaging.

"Saw this bathroom at a showing today. What do you think? Are pink tile bathrooms making a comeback?"

You would be surprised how many people have strong opinions about retro, colored tile bathrooms. My cousin Jackie fell in love with a house partly because of a sunshine yellow tile bathroom. This is a great way to get your audience talking. Also, notice how "showing" was slipped in there. Not only will people pay attention this post, but they will be gently reminded that you are in the real estate business.

Be Yourself

The best way to be engaging is to use your personality, unless you don't have one. In that case, just make one up! My followers know that I am a techie and a foodie with a wickedly sarcastic, sometimes irreverent, sense of humor who loves cats and stays far away from children. That gives me a lot upon which to build. The one caveat, as always, be careful not to offend a potential customer. The fact of the matter is that people think I'm funny... at least most of the time. I'd be foolish to not capitalize on that!

An example of a simple post that got quite a bit of attention was a photo I snapped driving down the freeway in New Orleans, LA. I know, I shouldn't be using my phone while driving, but this was too good. There was a large truck in front of me with the words "Coastal Erection" emblazoned across the back. My caption was a simple, "Why????"

Sometimes, being funny is all you need. Don't be afraid to let your personality shine through.

Adding Value

Once you move beyond simply having fun and engaging your audience, it's time to focus on trying to add value to your Instagram content. This can present a little more of a challenge for some. However, with a little creativity, some ideas can come to mind.

Community Focus

Using Instagram can be a great way to spotlight community events or information. Perhaps you see a poster for an upcoming play at the local theater or a sign advertising the neighborhood garage sale next weekend. Take a picture and post it. Be the resource people look to when they need to know what is going on in the community.

DIY Projects

Maybe you are crafty or handy around the house. Take photos of projects before, during, and after. This can also include cooking. If people like what they see, they may just ask you how you accomplished this feat. Helping someone simplify their life is an amazing way to build rapport and stay top-of-mind.

Boosting Your Reach

There are several different ways to spread your cheer beyond the borders of Instagram and to increase your followers. The first is sharing on other sites. This goes back to the topic of Cohesion. Cross promoting your platforms will increase the bang-for-your-buck. This is done seamlessly with the push of a button when the post is created. You simply select the Facebook, Twitter, Tumblr, Flickr, or Swarm buttons to share the photo on any or all the platforms you choose.

Next, you can start using hashtags. For the old-school bunch, it's the pound symbol, or tic-tac-toe board. Hashtags are a great way to categorize your content. People follow certain topics and will actually start following you with the right hashtags. Here is a recent example of a random share that gleaned several followers from varying backgrounds, quite unintentionally!

Recently, I rented a car for one of my many work trips. I was none too impressed with the mustard-yellow Kia Soul they gave me.

My post read: "My ride for the next 3 days. Mustard is TOTALLY my color lol. #bigpimpin #roadwarrior #rentalcar #sarcasm"

Within minutes, I had several new followers. One of which was someone in Savannah, GA, who runs some rental car agency. The hashtag drew attention! On another note, the car was actually quite comfy, and I never lost it in a parking lot!

Much like Facebook, Instagram has a tagging feature. If you are with someone else, tag them in your post and their audience will see it too! It's a great way to achieve an instant reach boost. You can also tag someone whose attention you want to get. Either way will accomplish the goal. Just be sure that the photo doesn't contain anything that the person you tag might find objectionable. For example, some people don't like to be photographed with a drink in their hand or at a certain location. Just be sensitive to that fact before tagging the whole world.

Instagram is an incredible way to boost your name recognition. It's also fun and easy to operate. Just download the app, connect it with your Facebook account, and off you go! The second step is not absolutely necessary, but I highly recommend it! You can even attach it to a Facebook Business Page. Either way, be sure to cross-promote!

Pinterest

Some of you might be thinking, "Pinterest? I am not interested in building a dog house out of popsicle sticks or weaving a throw rug!" Believe it or not, Pinterest is so much more than just arts and crafts. It's a collection of millions of links to content you didn't even know existed. The best part is that it is actually useful information that can enhance your marketing efforts.

Pinterest is basically just a giant collection of hyperlinks and article descriptions embedded within a photo. It's a highly visual platform. Content creation becomes even more challenging on Pinterest because you are trying to grab the visual attention of the user. Headlines are also important. The goal is to get re-pinned and for them to click on your photo, linking them to your original site. The more interesting you are; the more activity you can expect.

Pinterest began primarily in the arts and crafts arena. Fans of DIY projects would get and share ideas about all sorts of topics. As the user base grew, so did the list of topics. Now you can find information on a ridiculous number of subjects from countless sources. While the Pinterest user base is still skewed toward the female persuasion, those numbers are equalizing more and more as time goes on. It's a site for anyone and everyone!

Mining for Content

This is probably my most popular use for Pinterest. So many people WANT to create a rock solid social media plan, but just can't bring themselves to making the time to find content on a weekly basis. The task can seem daunting at times. With Pinterest, you can spend as little as a few minutes at a time searching for pertinent articles for your plan. Chances are that you will spend more than a few minutes because Pinterest, like Facebook, is highly addictive. If you don't want to actually maintain a Pinterest presence, you can just create secret boards that only you can see. Use various boards to keep things organized. That way, when the time comes to publish, all you need to do is pick an article you like and use it.

Marketing with Pinterest

Personally, I think once you see your secret boards bulging with content, you will feel confident enough to unleash your genius upon the world! It's really not that hard. Your boards are your niches. If you are marketing yourself as an interior design/staging expert, have a board about that. If you are targeting For Sale by Owner properties, have a board for sellers. You get the point? Just be sure to add new and interesting content on a regular basis.

When to Post

Knowing what to post is pretty easy. Posting correctly and at the right times can be a little trickier. The overall consensus from Pinterest experts like Bill Gassett, one of my favorite social media bloggers, is to spread your posts out leaving about 60 minutes between them. According to a post Bill wrote for the National Association of REALTORS Young Professionals Network blog site, YPN Lounge[1], "You won't annoy your followers, and you'll spread out your presence over the course of the day." That's when your secret boards can come into play again. Save them up and pin at the right moment. It's so easy to get caught up in the frenzy and excitement of finding amazing content. I have even been guilty of that offense. Use some restraint and your followers will thank you.

The thing to remember about Pinterest is that it is visual! Just be sure your content will catch the eye of your intended audience and you should be fine. I will repeat my warning that Pinterest is highly addictive. You need to have a plan or else you may find yourself wasting countless hours wading through interesting, but useless content. You have been warned!

1 – Gassett, Bill. (2015, April 23). The Biggest Social Media Fails in Real Estate. Retrieved from http://ypnlounge.blogs.realtor.org/2015/04/23/the-biggest-social-media-fails-in-real-estate/

Chapter 5: Points to Remember

Now that we have covered the major points of social media management, it's time to reiterate some of the finer nuances of a successful campaign. Simply blasting out content will only get you so far. You have to start your social media journey with not only a plan, but a mindset. If you remember these points, you will have a much more positive result!

It's Not All About You!

This is probably the hardest lesson for a salesperson to learn. We are trained from day one about self-promotion. "If you don't toot your horn, no one else will." That mantra was pounded into my brain from the moment I entered the world of real estate. Before you freak out, I am not speaking out against self-promotion. It's still an integral part of any business plan. However, when it comes to social media planning, a self-centered approach is the quickest path to obscurity.

Know Your Audience

Remember, your goal is to create likeable and shareable content. Simply talking about yourself is the opposite of that. Your focus must be on your audience.

Put yourself in their shoes. Ask, "If I were <insert target criteria>, what would be important to me?" If you can't answer that simple question, maybe you shouldn't have chosen that niche. Your content should say to them, "I know you, and I know what's important to you." Your audience must feel that everything you do is for their benefit alone. People will do business with someone they know, like, and trust. The fastest way to build trust is to understand your target and speak their language.

Neutrality is Key

Your personal opinions on matters outside the business world should never pollute your social media marketing efforts. Your goal is to add value and enhance the lives of your audience. I fail to see how your opinion of a political figure or your interpretation of a religious doctrine will accomplish that task. This is also true of your opinion of a competitor. Some people might test you to see if you are the type to badmouth your "enemies." Don't fall into that trap. If you are in sales, you must learn to play things close to the vest. Every person you meet is a potential client. Don't assume they agree with you.

Let Your Personality Shine Through

You are a unique and special individual, just like everybody else. It's hard to stand out as singular among thousands. Your social media efforts can show people your style, sense of humor, soft side, or your marketing genius. However, you must learn ways to subtly weave this into your value-added content. Personally, I use humor to connect with my audience. Whatever your strength may be, use it to your advantage!

Your passion should be your guide. Whatever lights a fire in your belly can lead you to the focus of your marketing. People are naturally drawn to others like them. When your interests align, great relationships can be forged!

Have Fun!

If you don't enjoy using social media, just don't. People can see right through your weak attempt at pretending. It's not something everyone should do. It's simply a tool in the box. The good news is that if you DO want to learn, there are people who can either teach you or do it for you. Social media is meant to be enjoyable. Believe it or not, you can have fun AND reach your audience!

Stay Positive

No one likes a sad sack! This may seem pretty obvious. However, I wouldn't be doing my job if I didn't mention it. When was the last time you thought, *"Gee, I really wish I could hang out with that crabby guy that complains all the time!"* My guess is probably never. We just instinctively avoid people who darken our moods. The same is true on social media as it is in real life. You may not notice it right away, but if you are constantly in a bad mood or display a downtrodden personality, people will begin to avoid you or even unfriend you. There is no effective way to build an audience when no one wants to interact with you.

If you are in sales and don't know how to put a positive spin on even the worst news, I have to question your career choice. Imagine a local industry is laying off hundreds of people. What good will it do to run around like Chicken Little claiming the sky is falling? Find the silver lining. More listing inventory means lower prices. Lower prices will entice more buyers into the market. Shift your focus to buyers and tell them what a great time it is to buy! That's just one example of how you can avoid being a dark cloud of doom.

Conclusion

Here we are at the end of our journey. We have covered a lot of ground together, but even that is only the tiniest fraction of the information available. Social Media is an ever-changing, ever-expanding world. No one can claim to know everything there is to know about every platform. I certainly don't make such a claim.

I hope you have gained even the simplest morsel of knowledge. I consider myself to be a lifetime learner and have come to appreciate the value of "nuggets of knowledge." It is my desire that this book will ignite the spark of interest that was there before you read it. I hope that spark grows into a flame that spurs you on to dig deeper for more information and to commit to creating an amazing social media marketing campaign.

If you have learned something valuable, or have questions about anything specific, I would love to hear from you! Feel free to email me at feedback@cronusmediaventures.com.

I welcome comments, questions, and especially success stories!

I wish you the best as you continue on your quest for knowledge.